Wilma Rudolph Gold-Medal Winner

Peter Baer

INFOMAX COMMON CORE READERS

Rosen Classroom™

New York

Published in 2014 by The Rosen Publishing Group, Inc.
29 East 21st Street, New York, NY 10010

Book Design: Mickey Harmon

Photo Credits: Cover, pp. 7, 15 ASSOCIATED PRESS/AP Images.com; p. 5 Jerry Cooke/Contributor/Sports Illustrated/Getty Images; p. 9 CDC/Wikipedia.org; p. 11 Mark Kauffmam/Contributor/TIME & LIFE Images/Getty Images; p. 13 Mondadori/Contributor/Mondadori/Getty Images; p. 17 David Lees/Contributor/TIME & LIFE Images/Getty Images; p. 21 Hulton Archive/Stringer/Getty Images Sport/Getty Images; p. 22 sunsetman/Shutterstock.com.

ISBN: 978-1-4777-2381-4
6-pack ISBN: 978-1-4777-2383-8

Manufactured in the United States of America

CPSIA Compliance Information: Batch #CS13RC: For further information contact Rosen Publishing, New York, New York at 1-800-237-9932.

Contents

Who Was Wilma Rudolph?

Do you know who Wilma Rudolph was? She was a famous **athlete**. Her best sport was running. She was a track and field star, and even won gold medals at the **Olympics**!

Wilma Rudolph was so fast that people called her the fastest woman in the world. Wilma became famous when she was only 16 years old. It took a lot of work to get there.

A medal is a piece of metal you get for winning something. Wilma Rudolph won three gold medals at the Olympics!

U.S.A
117
133

Wilma was born in St. Bethlehem, Tennessee, on June 23, 1940. The Rudolph family was really big. There were 22 children! Wilma was the third youngest.

Wilma was born earlier than she was supposed to be. Since she was premature (pree-muh-CHUR), her body wasn't very strong. This affected her health throughout her early childhood.

Wilma was sickly as a child. She was sick with scarlet fever, polio, and other serious illnesses.

Wilma Rudolph

A Sickly Child

In the 1940s and 1950s, many children in the United States were sick with a virus called polio. Wilma got polio when she was 4. It hurt her left leg and foot, and almost made her unable to use them.

Wilma wore a brace and special shoes for 5 years to fix her leg and foot. Many doctors told her she would never walk again.

Leg braces were used to keep a person's legs and feet in the right position.

Wilma dealt with other illnesses besides polio. At the time, African Americans weren't able to go to the best hospitals and doctors. Her family didn't have a lot of money, either. However, they still did everything they could to help her get better.

Because she was so unhealthy, nobody thought Wilma would ever become an athlete. But Wilma was naturally talented. She just needed to be discovered.

Wilma Rudolph was naturally good at sports. Do you know which ones she played?

U.S.

Basketball Star

By age 11, Wilma's leg and foot were better. She joined her school's basketball team. Wilma loved basketball, and she was very good at it! She set many state records in high school basketball.

When Wilma was in tenth grade, Ed Temple, a track **coach** from Tennessee State University (TSU), went to her basketball game. He saw how good she was and wanted her to run for his team.

Even though he only saw her play basketball, Ed Temple could tell Wilma would be a great runner.

Ed Temple
Wilma Rudolph

Who Was Ed Temple?

Meeting Ed Temple changed Wilma's life. He became her coach. Because of Ed, Wilma joined the summer track team at TSU. She trained with the college team for 2 years, even though she was still in high school.

Wilma was so fast that she went to the Summer Olympics in Melbourne, Australia, in 1956. She was only 16 years old! She won a bronze medal.

Do you know what a relay is? It's a race that's run by a team of people. Wilma and her team won a bronze medal for a 4x100 relay race.

A
B

After the Olympics, Wilma finished high school and went to college at TSU. She wanted to go to the Olympics again, but this time she wanted to win a gold medal.

Four years later, she went to the 1960 Summer Olympic Games in Rome, Italy. As a young African American woman, this was a big deal! The whole world was watching to see what she could do.

Wilma went to the Olympics twice, at ages 16 and 20.

An Olympic Star

Wilma was the star of the 1960 Summer Olympics. Her first event was the 100-meter dash, which she ran in only 11 seconds! Then, she ran the 200-meter dash in 23.2 seconds.

A few days later, Wilma and her teammates ran the 400-meter relay in 44.5 seconds. She broke world records for all these events. She was the first American woman to win three gold medals in track and field during a single Olympic Games.

After these races, people called Wilma the fastest woman in history.

Wilma's Races

KEY

100 meter	yellow arrow
200 meter	blue arrow
400 meter	purple arrow
finish line	black line

Race 1: 11 seconds

Race 2: 23.2 seconds

Race 3: 44.5 seconds

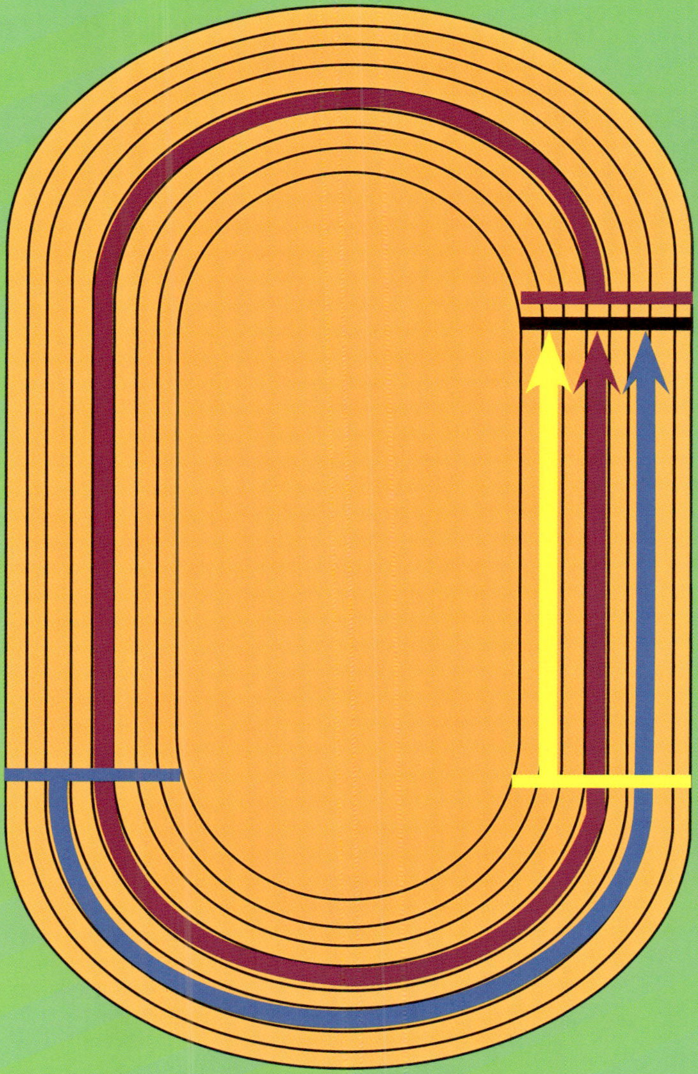

When Wilma returned to the United States, her town wanted to have a parade for her. She said she wouldn't go unless both blacks and whites could attend. It was the first **integrated** event in her city.

Wilma retired from racing in 1962. She spent the rest of her life **promoting** sports. She created the Wilma Rudolph Foundation to help young athletes and also worked as a track coach.

In Wilma's day, blacks and whites often had to do things in different places at different times. This changed in the 1960s.

U.S.A
ITAL
BRI

A Hero to All

Over the course of her life, Wilma received many awards for her accomplishments. Wilma died on November 17, 1994, at age 54. People all over the world were sad.

Today, we remember Wilma Rudolph as a hero. Even though she had a hard childhood, she became one of the best athletes in American sports history!

Glossary

athlete (ATH-leet) A person who has trained to be very good at a sport.

coach (KOHCH) A person who trains or teaches others.

integrated (IHN-tuh-gray-tuhd) Marked by allowing blacks and whites together.

Olympics (uh-LIHM-pihks) A series of international sporting events held once every two years.

promote (pruh-MOHT) To make other people interested in what you're interested in.

Index